WHY WAS THERE AN AMERICAN REVOLUTION?

History Non Fiction Books for Grade 3 | Children's History Books

Speedy Publishing LLC

40 E. Main St. #1156

Newark, DE 19711

www.speedypublishing.com

Copyright 2017

In this book, we're going to talk about the reasons why the American Revolution happened. So, let's get right to it!

When people revolt against a government, there are many events over a long period of time that bring them to that point. The colonies that were established in North America were under British rule until the American Revolution. After the colonies won the American Revolution, they declared themselves to be a new government and the United States was born.

WHY DID PEOPLE LEAVE ENGLAND AND COME TO AMERICA?

★ ★ ★

It wasn't easy to travel to America from Europe in the 1600s, so people that decided to come to America were taking a big risk. America was not yet heavily populated except for the Native Americans. The pilgrims who came to America in 1620 were leaving Europe because they wanted to be free from religious persecution.

PILGRIMS MEET NATIVE AMERICANS

However, as the colonies became established in America, little by little the British started to get more involved with how they were governed. Americans were very independent-minded pioneers and they didn't like that the government was trying to control them. They wanted to keep their hard-won freedoms.

It's true that the American colonies were part of Britain. However, they had had their own governing bodies over 150 years by this time. One of the freedoms that the British wanted to restrict was their ability to move westward. Americans were pioneers and they were upset that anyone could control their desire to move west across the continent. The other pressing issue was that Britain was now starting to tax them heavily.

THE VICTORY OF MONTCALM'S TROOPS

THE FRENCH AND INDIAN WAR

The British were not the only ones who owned land in America. The French had also come to America and had seized land. The French and British were fighting with each other in Europe as well as fighting over their territories in America. Finally, the British had had enough.

They wanted to drive France out of America. The colonists and the British aligned themselves with some Native Americans to fight the French. The French did the same and rallied other Native Americans to join forces with them.

The French and Indian War, which was called the Seven Years' War in Europe even though it lasted for nine years, was begun in 1754 and ended in 1763.

After the war was over, the British still had troops that were stationed in the colonies for protection. Keeping troops in the Americas was expensive. The war both in Europe and the Americas had cost the British a lot of money.

They started to levy taxes to get money that the British government needed. The citizens in Europe were already heavily taxed so the British began to enact laws that would tax the colonists.

SEARCH WARRANTS ON SHIPS

Ship inspectors located in England had long had the responsibility to inspect ships that were traveling to the colonies, but they weren't doing this very actively until around 1760. Now violators were immediately prosecuted and did not even get a trial by jury.

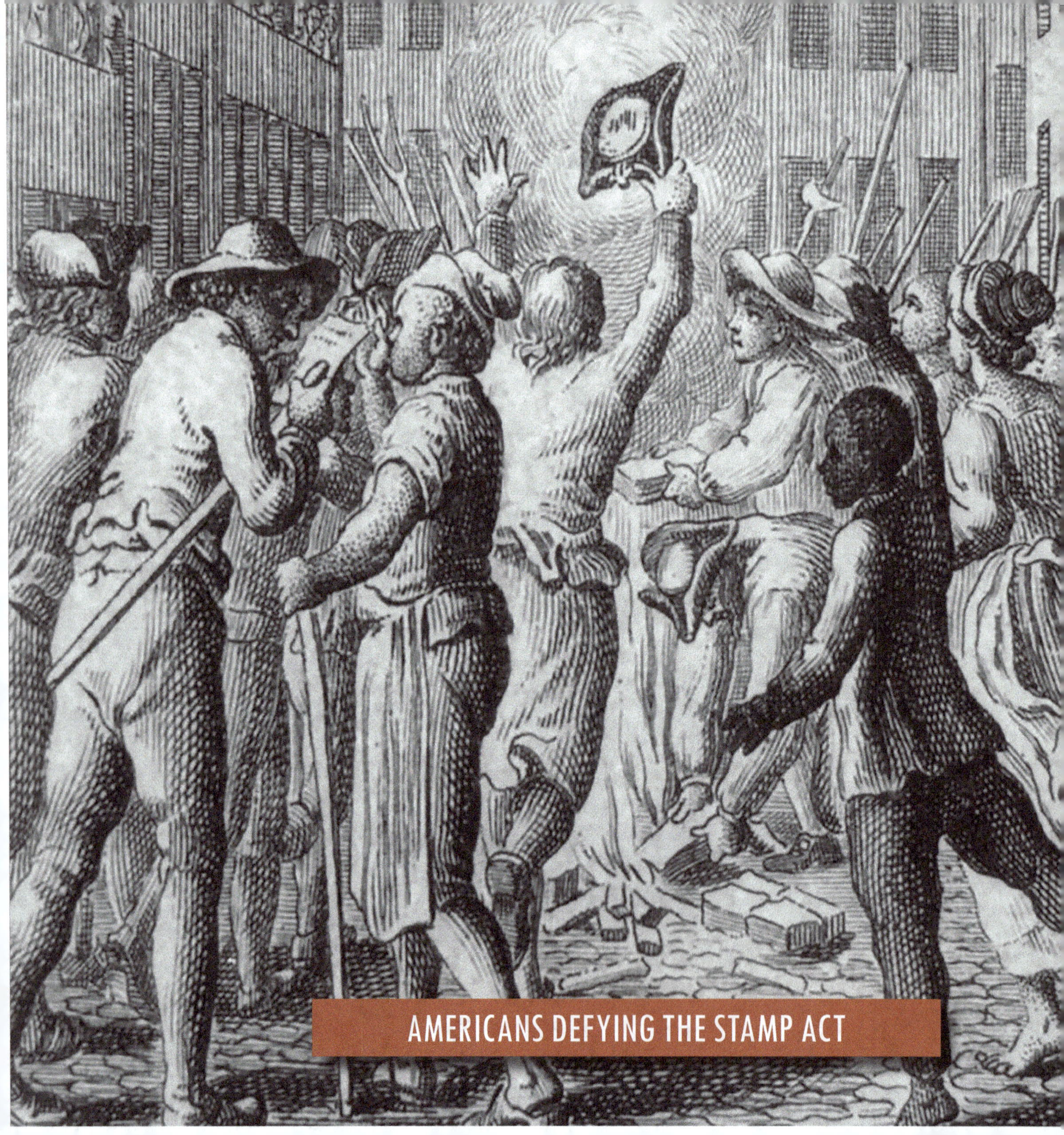

AMERICANS DEFYING THE STAMP ACT

TAXES, TAXES, TAXES

Before 1764, the British had left the colonists alone to govern themselves for the most part. Then, they started to impose new tax laws one after the other. They established The Sugar Act, then the Currency Act, followed by the Quartering Act, and the Stamp Act.

THE SUGAR ACT AND THE CURRENCY ACT

In 1764, these acts were established so that the British could collect taxes at ports. Since these were levied on the goods that business owners were shipping, the ordinary citizen didn't really see the taxation because it was frequently absorbed into the price of the goods. Many business owners found ways to avoid the taxes, but this was the beginning of some serious tension between the colonists and their parent country.

OF THE TOWN OF BOSTON IN NEW-ENGLAND AND BRITISH SHIPS
ENGLAND
B
A
3
4
5

BOSTONIANS READING THE STAMP ACT

THE STAMP ACT OF 1765

The Stamp Act of 1765 brought even more taxes to the colonists. Now, every single piece of paper was taxed. It wasn't bad enough that legal documents and newspapers were taxed. Even decks of playing card were taxed! There was an official stamp that indicated whether the taxes had been paid on these documents. This is why this act was called the "Stamp Act."

The colonists were more than outraged over these taxes. England, their parent country, didn't see the problem. Why were the colonists complaining? What they were being asked to pay was much less of an amount than the British citizens were paying. The money raised by the act wasn't even enough to cover 1/3 of the operating cost of keeping the British troops in America for the colonists' safety.

STAMP ACT RIOT

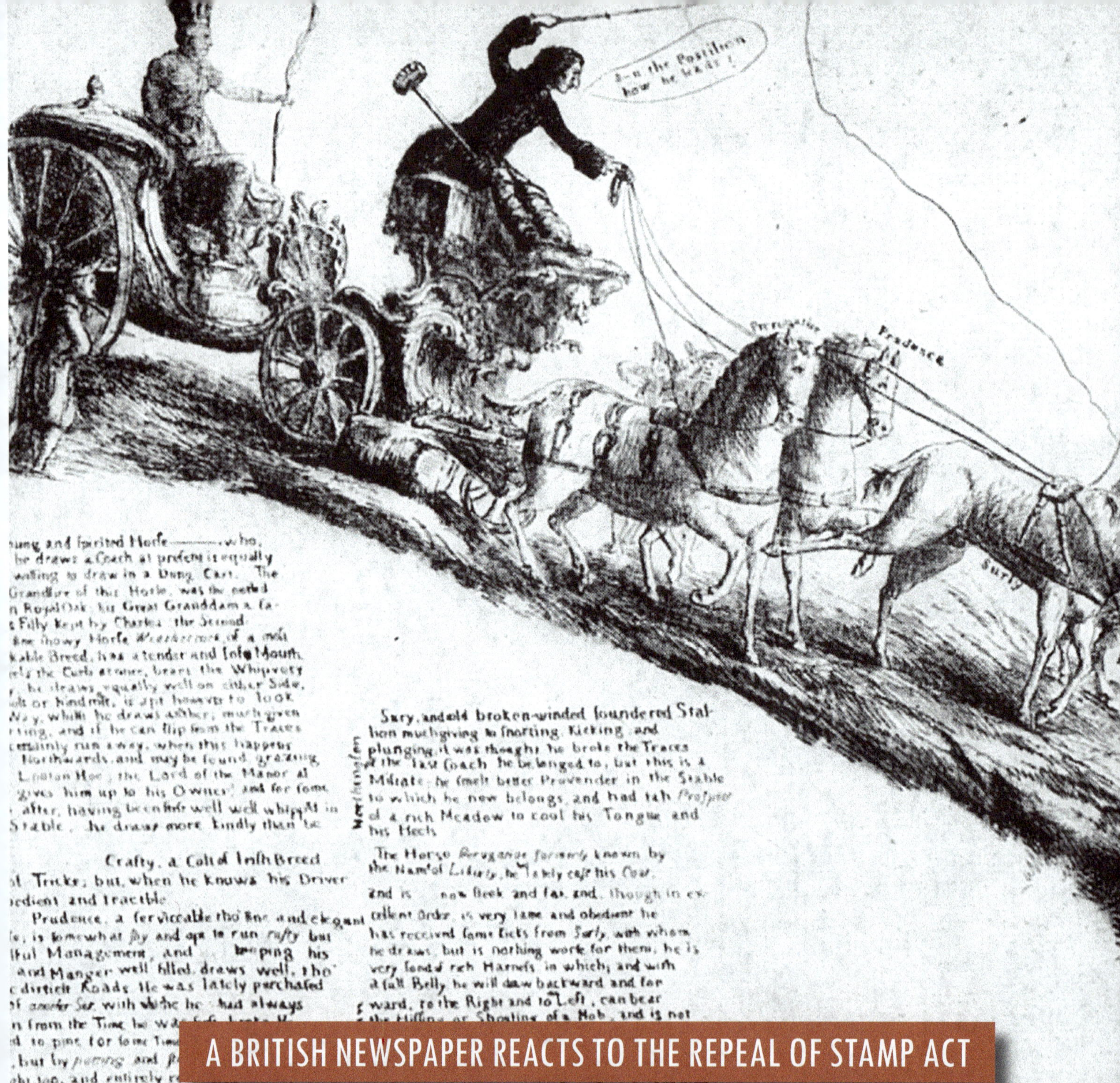

A BRITISH NEWSPAPER REACTS TO THE REPEAL OF STAMP ACT

WHY DID THE COLONISTS HATE THE STAMP ACT?

The people in the British colonies in America did not understand the need for British troops now that the threat from France was gone. Why should they have to continue to pay for keeping British troops in America? They knew that the citizens living in England were paying even more, but shouldn't the taxation on them be less since their circumstances were different.

After all, in order to remain in America, they had to clear land and fight off Native Americans. Since they had set foot in America in 1620, many colonists had died building the colonies and establishing civilization in America to give further glory to the British Empire. These taxes seemed like the final insult. They refused to pay them!

Semper Eadem
Thro' faults &c.
All of a Stamp
The Sh...
Liverpool Goods
Manchester
Halifax
Leeds
105

CLARA

Furthermore, the citizens in England had representation in Parliament so they could air any grievances. The colonists did not have anyone representing them in Parliament. They began to rally the cry "No Taxation Without Representation."

The colonists began to violently protest by not paying the taxes. They threatened those who were collecting the taxes. So much so that some of these individuals quit their jobs in fear.

They took the papers to the streets and burned them. They boycotted the products of British merchants. They wouldn't go into their stores or purchase their goods.

The colonists started to organize. In 1765, they had a meeting in New York City during the month of October. During this Stamp Act Congress they created a written protest to send to the British government.

THE N.Y. TRIBUNE
THE NATION
REPUBLICAN
AND
DEMOCRATIC PAPERS
BROOKLYN EAGLE
BOSTON POST
THE WORLD
VETO

WHO WERE THE SONS OF LIBERTY?

As tensions with Britain grew, groups of American patriots were organized. They called themselves the Sons of Liberty. They became a very influential group during the American Revolution. Their protests started to hurt the British merchants.

Eventually, Britain did away with the Stamp Act, but they passed the Declaratory Act, which re-emphasized that they had the right to pass laws and collect taxes whether the colonists had representation in Parliament or not!

THE QUARTERING ACT AND THE TOWNSHEND ACT

In 1765, the British Parliament passed the Quartering Act, which outlined how British troops in America were to find room and board. The act required that the colonies provide barracks to house the British soldiers. If there were not enough barracks, the colonists had to provide other lodging for the soldiers.

The colonists didn't want the soldiers around at all and now they were being told that they must find places for the soldiers to live and to sleep. When the colonists refused to cooperate, the British passed a law that basically didn't allow the governor of the state of New York to sign any legislation into law until the Quartering Act had been followed.

THOMAS GAGE

In 1767, the Townshend Acts were passed by Parliament and imports of paper, glass, tea, lead, and paint were to be taxed. These additional taxes were causing more and more unrest in the colonies. The colonists were beginning to talk about starting a revolt against the British.

CHARLES TOWNSHEND

THE BOSTON MASSACRE

In 1770, in Boston, Massachusetts, a British officer who was unable to find suitable quarters for his soldiers had them pitch tents on Boston Common, which is the central plaza area in Boston.

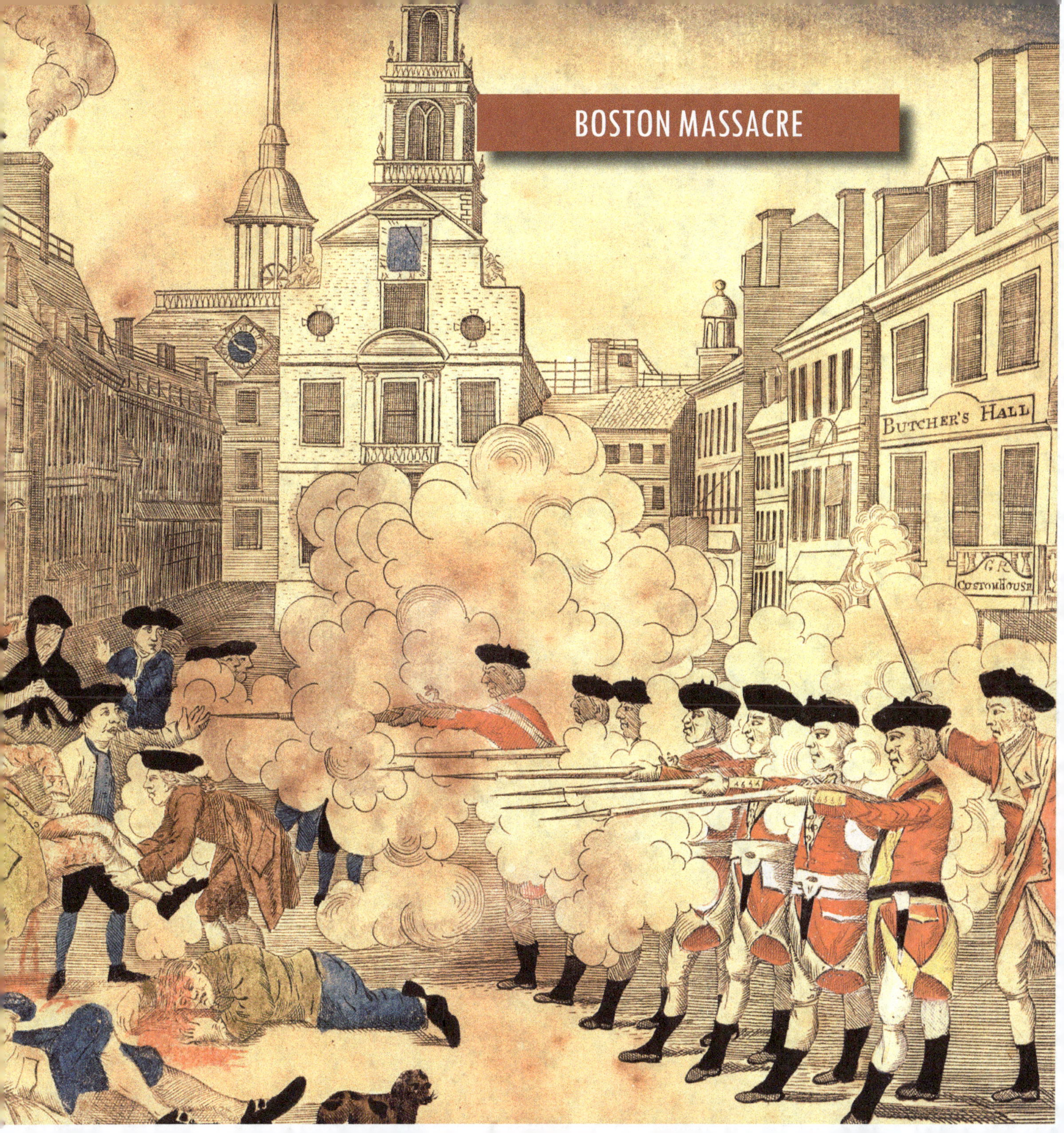
BOSTON MASSACRE
BUTCHER'S HALL
CUSTOM HOUSE

The soldiers were now in close quarters with the patriots and there were street brawls started that escalated into violence. The soldiers were provoked and opened fire killing several colonists.

THE BOSTON TEA PARTY

Three years later, the British levied a new tax. This time it was on tea. Several Boston patriots, dressed in disguise as Mohawk Indians, protested the tax by dumping the tea off the ship and into the waters of Boston harbor. This event was called the "Boston Tea Party."

BOSTON TEA PARTY

FIVE INTOLERABLE ACTS—ALLUSION TO BOSTON TEA PARTY

THE INTOLERABLE ACTS

The British wanted the colonies to be punished for throwing the tea overboard. They created a whole new group of laws that the patriots labeled "intolerable."

One of these acts closed the harbor in Boston, which caused problems both for patriots and for those who still supported the British government. These actions only made the colonies organize and unite together to fight the British.

BOSTON TEA PARTY MUSEUM

The American Revolution began on April 19, 1775 when fighting broke out between the British and the Patriots at the Battle of

Lexington. The fight for independence had finally begun.

Awesome! Now you know more about the events that led up to the American Revolution. You can find more American History books from Baby Professor by searching the website of your favorite book retailer.

Visit

BABY PROFESSOR
EDUCATION KIDS

www.BabyProfessorBooks.com
to download Free Baby Professor eBooks
and view our catalog of new and exciting
Children's Books

www.ingramcontent.com/pod-product-compliance
Lightning Source LLC
Chambersburg PA
CBHW082101130726

48003CB00009BA/2955